CW01647833

The day Jean-Pierre went round the world

Also by Paul Gallico in Piccolo

The Adventures of Jean-Pierre
The Day Jean-Pierre Joined the Circus
Manxmouse

Paul Gallico

The day JEAN-PIERRE went round the world

illustrated by Gioia Fiammenghi

Piccolo Pan Books

First published 1965 by William Heinemann Ltd
This edition published 1977 by Pan Books Ltd,
Cavaye Place, London SW10 9PG

ISBN 0 330 24357 8
Printed in Great Britain by
Richard Clay (The Chaucer Press) Ltd, Bungay, Suffolk

to
Susannah
Clench

chapter one

For weeks and weeks Cecile Durand had been dreaming of their annual fortnight's holiday in Paris and telling Jean-Pierre all about it. Now she and her father and mother were actually at Nice airport. It was beginning.

'You mustn't worry,' Cecile had whispered to Jean-Pierre, 'it won't be more than an hour in the aeroplane. Everyone has promised to take the best care of you.'

Jean-Pierre was Cecile's pet Guinea Pig and he was in a little wooden travelling box. It had a wire screen window for him to look out of and get air.

The box was well supplied with tags and labels to make *sure* that nothing could go wrong during the time when Jean-Pierre would be away from Cecile. He was to travel in the special place for animals in the baggage compartment of the Caravelle that was to take the family to Paris.

There was a label: MADEMOISELLE CECILE DURAND, C/O MADAME LOUISE TISSAUD, 3 BIS RUE DE GRENELLE, PARIS 7. Madame Tissaud was Cecile's aunt whom they visited every year for two weeks in July.

Another label read: ABYSSINIAN GUINEA PIG. DELICATE. DO NOT DROP.

Further ones commanded: THIS SIDE UP; FRAGILE; HANDLE WITH CARE; LIVESTOCK. And IN CASE OF ACCIDENT PLEASE INFORM: MLLE CECILE DURAND, C/O AUNT LOUISE TISSAUD, 3 BIS RUE DE GRENELLE, PARIS 7, FRANCE.

And then, besides, there were the secret instructions inside the little cage. No one but Cecile knew about these. This was just should anything go wrong.

But this, as her father had told her, was quite impossible. The fat jolly baggage man, who weighed the

cases of the Durands at the airport, assured Cecile that he would pass the word along for everyone to be extra careful with her pet.

'There, you see, Mademoiselle,' he said, 'he's all properly labelled for Paris. Don't bid him goodbye, but say *au revoir*. Before you know it, he'll be safely returned to you.'

Even so, it had been an unhappy moment when the man took Jean-Pierre and placed him on the scales with their other luggage. The Guinea Pig had squeaked, sneezed and pressed his pink nose against the wire of his window. Cecile felt that, in spite of all her promises to him that he would be perfectly safe, he looked worried.

But this was understandable, since Jean-Pierre had

never made a trip before in a travelling box, much less flown in an aeroplane.

When all of the bags had been weighed, checked and tagged, they were placed upon a moving belt and away they sailed behind the counter, turned a corner and then disappeared down an incline.

By craning her neck, Cecile saw the last of Jean-Pierre's nose and bright golden eyes. She hoped he was enjoying himself, and thought what fun it would be to ride on one of those moving bands herself.

Well, she had really done all she could to ensure his safety and comfort.

An airport was a most interesting and exciting place, Cecile thought. People were coming and going, carrying bags of every size and shape. Showcases were filled with the most fascinating things for sale, not to mention the selection of sweets at the newspaper stall. There was the roar and whine of jet engines. Loudspeakers announced departures and arrivals of flights to and from the most far-off and thrilling places.

Most children when they think of a holiday look forward to going to the country and playing in the woods; or to paddling at the seashore, finding shells, or digging in the sand. But Cecile *lived* in the country, not far from the sea. Her father owned a flower farm behind Cannes, which is on the Mediterranean. There he raised the most beautiful roses and carnations. This was Cecile's home with her pets – a dog named Bobi, a cat called Coco and a rabbit, Gris-Gris. And, of course, her own very special pet was Jean-Pierre whom she loved more than anything or anyone, next to her father and mother. She had bought him herself with her pocket-money.*

Her holiday was just the other way round. It was to journey to a city where:

(1) Her aunt had a house. It was a tall, old building and from her room on the top floor Cecile could look out over the rooftops and chimney pots of Paris. Here was a new and different kind of world where one could imagine the most extraordinary things happening.

(2) Her aunt also had a wonderful library, full of marvellous books. Many of them had interesting pictures. When it rained, as it almost always did for one or two days, Cecile was allowed to go in there and look at them.

(3) And then, of course, there were all of the thrilling and *different* things one could do in Paris, such as eating out in restaurants. They might go for a ride on the *Bateau Mouche*, the sightseeing boat that journeys on the Seine. She also liked walking with her mother down the Champs-Elysées and looking in the shop windows. And then there were such absolutely splendid treats as visiting Versailles, or Montmartre, or going up the Eiffel Tower in a lift and actually having lunch there.

This year, however, as the time for the holiday had approached, Cecile's parents noticed that she was more quiet than usual. She did not chatter so much about it and seemed to be worried.

* *The Adventures of Jean-Pierre*, also in Piccolo

After several attempts, Madame Durand had been able to get to the bottom of this. It was Jean-Pierre.

Ever since the little Guinea Pig had been kidnapped, or rather pignapped, by the butcher's boy* and returned only through the cleverness in sending Cecile a message, Jean-Pierre had been allowed to sleep in Cecile's room. He had a special cage there and the two had been more inseparable than ever. Much as Cecile loved the visit to her aunt, she was frightened at the thought of leaving Jean-Pierre behind.

It was different with Bobi, Coco and Gris-Gris. Nobody really would bother to steal a farm dog, or a house cat, or a barn rabbit. Besides, there were the gardeners to look after them while the Durands were away. But an Abyssinian Guinea Pig with golden-yellow eyes, black and brown rough-haired fur, and one who was magic as well, was not the same.

It was the first time that Cecile was torn between love for her pet and something she very much wanted. She did not know what to do and needed help.

Like all good mothers who love their children more than themselves, Madame Durand took Cecile's problem upon her own shoulders. Without saying anything, she consulted her husband.

Monsieur Durand, like many fathers, fussed and fumed at first and was difficult. To carry along a Guinea Pig with their luggage would be a nuisance. A box would have to be bought. There would be the extra weight. Madame Tissaud might very well put her foot down (for Cecile's

* *The Adventures of Jean-Pierre*

aunt was *his* sister) about having a Guinea Pig brought into her home.

In short, he raised all of the objections his wife expected he would, but in the end he agreed to write and ask.

To his astonishment, a letter came back, 'If it will make the child happy, I have no objection.'

And so one day, Madame Durand was able to say to her daughter, 'I have a surprise for you, Cecile. I know you are worried about leaving Jean-Pierre behind. Well, we have arranged that you will be able to take him.'

And even Monsieur Durand was pleased and less grumpy. For Cecile squealed and jumped up and down with joy, and hugged them both. She said they were the best parents in the world.

Then there was more excitement when it came to the preparations, the finding and purchasing of a suitable box. Cecile held long conversations with Jean-Pierre, telling him all about what Paris was like.

There was only one small thing to mar Cecile's happiness. She had thought she would be able to carry Jean-Pierre's box on her lap, or Jean-Pierre himself in her pocket, as she often did. Monsieur Durand explained it was a rule of the airlines that no animals were permitted inside the cabin. He would have to go with the luggage. But since the flight to Paris was very short, Jean-Pierre would not mind.

'But what if he should be lost?' Cecile had asked.

'Between Nice and Paris? How could he be? The aeroplane doesn't stop. Come now, Cecile, we have arranged for you to have your little Guinea Pig with you on your holiday and you mustn't fuss. I will give an extra tip to the man at the baggage counter to make sure he's properly looked after. Jean-Pierre will be on the same aeroplane with us.'

With this Cecile had to be satisfied. But it was then that she decided to take her own precautions. She prepared special instructions in both French and English. But about these she told no one. The English translation was not very good, because it was only the second year that Cecile had studied the language at school. Nevertheless it was understandable. It read as follows:

Dear Anyone:

Please, this is my own Guinea Pig, Jean-Pierre, whom I love better than anyone, except my parents. He is an Abyssinian Guinea Pig. He is special. He is also magic and can understand. If he is lost, or misses the plane, or anything should happen, please do not leave him in his box but take him out and give him love. He is used to being cuddled at night and spoken to. He drinks milk, but likes it made a little warm for him, please. He eats anything from the garden like carrots, lettuce, cabbage, radishes, pieces of marrow, bits of apple, pear and grapes. Also crumbs of bread or cake, or a little cheese. But best of all he likes pomegranate seeds, if you have any. If not, it does not matter. Please do not give him too much, as he will make a pig of himself if you let him. He should be kept warm. If he sneezes it is not because he has a cold, but because he is excited. He has his big meal at supper time. That is all I have to say, except do not forget to give him lots of love and hugs and not let him be lonely.

Thank you very much,
Jean-Pierre's mother,
Cecile Durand

To this she added her address once more, care of Madame Tissaud. Cecile put the two letters in separate envelopes, addressed one in French and the other in English, TO WHOM IT MAY CONCERN. These she quietly attached to the inside of Jean-Pierre's travelling box the morning they left. They were driven to the airport by the head gardener who looked after things during Monsieur Durand's absence.

The loudspeaker went 'Plank, plonk, plink' and a voice announced, 'Passengers for Paris on flight 1200, proceed to gate 5. Please have your boarding-cards ready.'

Now the holiday and the real part of the trip was actually beginning.

By this time Cecile was so excited that she almost dropped the huge packet of carnations she was taking to her Aunt Louise. She kept tugging at her mother's arm to hurry her, so that they would be sure to get the best places.

There were many aeroplanes parked on the apron of the airport, but Cecile knew the Caravelle at once, for she had flown before. She was allowed to run ahead and up the stairs into the aircraft and occupy a seat by a window. Then, they were all strapped in and the sweet offered by

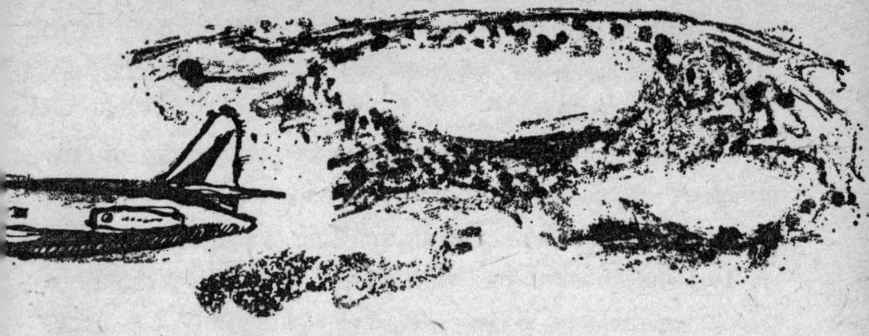

the air hostess popped into Cecile's mouth. They taxied to the end of the runway and with a great roar the jet plane thundered away and climbed into the sky.

Soon they were high over the Alpes Maritimes and Cecile looked down upon the little toy villages on the mountain tops. It was difficult for her to imagine the speed with which they were flying until she saw a tiny bus crawling on a winding road, far below. Now she remembered how long it took them in their car when they went for a drive in the hills. And in less than an hour they would be in Paris, about 400 miles away.

Then she gave herself up to dreaming about being reunited with Jean-Pierre, safe and sound in his little travelling box somewhere in one of the luggage compartments of the giant Caravelle.

Only alas, he wasn't!

At that moment the little Guinea Pig was indeed snug in his cage, but he was on an entirely different kind of aeroplane and flying in exactly the opposite direction.

How could such a thing have happened?

It was a case of too much kindness, too much fuss and too much care.

For the man behind the baggage counter had said to his helper, 'Keep an eye out for this fellow. Special job. Belongs to a little girl.'

The attendant had passed the word along to the checker, 'Easy with this one. And see that he isn't frightened. The owner is the daughter of a friend of mine.'

And the checker had told the loader, 'Now don't go throwing this one about. He's very valuable. Cost a fortune, this sort does.'

The result was that Jean-Pierre had indeed been handled as though he were a crate of eggs. Instead of being dumped on to the barrow, there was a man in a uniform cap to carry him out to the loading-bay. Here he was set carefully upon the ground to wait until all the bags had been put aboard. Then he would be stowed in the special compartment.

So there Jean-Pierre sat comfortably enough upon the tarmac, sniffing the strange smells, clicking his teeth together and chewing on a portion of pomegranate seeds. These had been put in by Cecile as an extra treat to keep him quiet. Occasionally he sneezed.

An official came by, looked down upon the box and examined one of the labels. It was the one which happened to say, ABYSSINIAN GUINEA PIG. HANDLE WITH CARE. He gave a whistle of half surprise, half alarm and looked up quickly to where a huge, four-engined jet Boeing 707 was just about to close its doors. Picking up the carrying case he ran over to it. There he shouted and made some signals.

A door underneath the plane was quickly reopened. A

brown hand reached down from within, took Jean-Pierre aboard and the door was shut again.

The pilot, high up in the window of his control cabin was quite dark-skinned and had a beard. He waved to the men below on the ground. They waved back at him. Then the plane rolled away and a few minutes later disappeared into the sky.

Back at the Caravelle no one saw what had happened. The man who had brought Jean-Pierre out thought the loaders had taken him aboard. The loaders thought that the man had put him inside. Thus, since nobody said anything, the Caravelle, too, closed its doors and flew off.

But poor Cecile, dreaming happily and now looking down upon the rich lands of the Rhône valley, did not know anything of this at all.

chapter two

‘Three – four – and the little one over there makes five,’ counted Monsieur Durand, as their cases appeared once more upon a moving belt at Orly airport, Paris. ‘And that’s the lot.’

‘But Jean-Pierre!’ cried Cecile, ‘It isn’t everything. Jean-Pierre isn’t here yet!’

‘Of course,’ said her father, ‘I’d forgotten. But he won’t be coming that way. Someone will be bringing him.’

He leaned across and spoke to the Baggage Master who confirmed that if indeed there was a live animal on board the plane, he would be delivered to them by hand.

And so they waited. But, of course, no one came.

Now Cecile’s father spoke to the man again. He explained how large the box was and about Jean-Pierre inside, and how it was labelled. The Baggage Master nodded and disappeared through a door. All the other cases had already been cleared and the passengers departed with them.

Cecile had a sick feeling in the middle of her stomach. Where was Jean-Pierre?

This time the wait was very long and in the meantime another plane arrived. New pieces of luggage appeared. Cecile kept watching them, hoping to see the familiar box with Jean-Pierre in it.

At last the Baggage Master came out. He said to Monsieur Durand, ‘I am very sorry. The men have searched thoroughly but there is no such cage on the aeroplane or anywhere. Perhaps it was left behind. We’ll inquire.’

Cecile burst into tears and threw herself sobbing into her mother's arms. 'Jean-Pierre! Jean-Pierre! He's lost! I'll *never* see him again!'

Her mother said, 'Ssh, darling, don't worry! Of course he is not lost. They will find him. Someone has just been stupid and mislaid him. He will be here in a moment now.'

But Cecile knew better. For thereafter there was one of those long drawn-out series of mysterious comings and goings, funny looks and whisperings exchanged, which tell children that the grown-ups are in a mess and don't know what to do.

The door of the baggage room kept opening and shutting with unhappy-looking men nipping in and out. Her father grew very red in the face. Officials with gold braid

on their uniforms arrived and talked with him to one side. New ones with even more gold on their caps appeared and stood about uneasily.

It seemed to Cecile as though she were in a nightmare. Instead of happily proceeding in a taxi to Aunt Louise's house where a splendid second breakfast would be waiting for them, here they were, still at the airport an hour after arrival, and no Jean-Pierre.

Monsieur Durand was angry with everyone now: with Cecile because she was sobbing so loudly that other passengers stared, and with the airline people for being so stupid as to mislay a Guinea Pig. He was cross with his wife for persuading him to bring Jean-Pierre along and with himself for being angry.

He said, 'Come, come Cecile! Don't cry! Pull yourself together and be a big girl. Jean-Pierre will be returned safely to you. The man says they are sending messages everywhere to find out what has happened. The moment Jean-Pierre is traced, he will be sent back in no time. There's nothing to worry about. This happens often on airlines. Ha, ha! There's even a joke about it: breakfast in Paris, lunch in New York, baggage in Tokyo.'

Cecile did not think this was funny, nor did the airline officials. No one laughed, but she stopped crying.

'If you will give us your telephone number,' the chief of the airline men promised, 'we will ring your little daughter the very first moment we have heard of Jean-Pierre's whereabouts.'

And with that they had to be satisfied. They collected their bags and took a taxi to Aunt Louise. When they arrived they found her also in a state because they were so delayed that she was certain that their aeroplane had fallen out of the sky.

It was a sad and dismal way to begin what had always been a gladsome holiday.

And, of course, neither that night nor the following morning was there any word from the airport.

Cecile had sat by the telephone all the day, except when called to meals. She had slept very badly. Once, dreaming that she heard the telephone, she had leaped out of bed. There were also false alarms when friends of her aunt rang.

The next day she resumed her watch by the instrument until finally, at ten o'clock, her father himself called Orly.

There was no news. Yes, yes, they already had several reports from distant airports but no sign of the missing Guinea Pig. And he was not at Nice either. As soon as there was some word they would let him know.

To all intents and purposes Jean-Pierre had vanished from the face of the earth and might as well be on the moon. And this was what Cecile found the hardest to bear, not knowing where he was or what might be happening to him. It was something quite different from the pignapping where it was certain there had been a thief. Detectives came and the police sent out alarms and posters with Jean-Pierre's picture. And after all, he was near enough then to be able to use his magic.

She was not at all sure that even his special magic would be strong enough to overcome the distances between the places to which aeroplanes flew.

But she tried now to be brave. Although her own holiday was ruined, she did not wish to spoil it for her parents. So she put up a good front, smiled and pretended that she was not worried. She went where they went and tried to enjoy doing what they did.

On the third morning she had the surprise of her life.

And it did not come over the telephone, after all. It arrived in a letter addressed to Cecile in a queer, wriggly handwriting. On the envelope was one of the most interesting stamps she had ever seen.

It was a lovely bluey-green in colour and had a picture of an aeroplane flying over some mountains. On it was also a portrait of an imposing-looking, bearded man in a military collar. There was a great deal of funny writing too, but one word that she could read, namely ETHIOPIA.

Her aunt handed it to her saying, 'My goodness, Cecile, you do have friends in strange places!'

Cecile took it and ran to her father. 'Look, look, Papa! I've got a letter! It's such a funny-looking one. It must be from Jean-Pierre.'

She opened and unfolded it. It was written in some kind of English, but not any she had ever seen before at school. 'Papa, I can't understand it, can you read it for me and tell me what it says?'

Monsieur Durand was a highly educated man who spoke a number of languages. His father had been a professor at the University in Paris. He took the letter and this is what he read:

Palase Gardins,
Addis Ababa,
Ethiopia

Dear Cecile Durand,

Plees exuse speling. I am just lurn Englesh in Government skoole. I am Amhara boy 13 yeer old with very importent father. He cheef gardner in Palase of glorios Emperer Haile Selassie God bles him.

Yur Guinea pig com by mistak to Addis Ababa becos it say he Abyssinian. Evry one lafing becos no one ever see one lik him before hear in Abyssinia. They giv to me to tak kare of bikos my father so importent man. I red yur leter in Englesh and giv him warm gaots gotes goots milk wich he lik and I kis him. In morning I tak him for wark in palase gardins. Lion of glorios Emperer com up and smeled at him. Jean-Pierre he smel rite bak. Lion of glorios one look surpriz and smel agen. Jean-Pierre he smel agen to. Lion of glorios emperer he fritend of Jean-Pierre and run away. Jean-Pierre very brave he not rund away. I lik Jean-Pierre and sory when he leev for plane go home. So I rite and tel to you. Good luk.

Yur litel Abysinnia frend,
Abo Tenawayo

Cecile was wild with excitement when her father had translated the letter for her and she made him read it again. Jean-Pierre's magic was still working. Even though *he* had not written to her, it was almost as though he had. Clever little pig! He had found someone to do it for him. How happy she was now that she had prepared the secret messages.

But Jean-Pierre in Africa! And meeting a lion and drinking goat's milk! There were so many things she wanted to know about that she could hardly wait to ask her papa. For Cecile knew from her geography lessons that Ethiopia, also called Abyssinia, was indeed in Africa though not exactly where.

But it was Monsieur Durand who asked the first question. 'What do you suppose the boy meant by saying that he had read your letter in English?'

Cecile then told him of how, just in case Jean-Pierre might be lost, she had written instructions on how to look after him and put them inside his box.

Her father smiled and said, 'That was clever of you.'

Cecile then asked, 'Where is Addis Ababa?'

'Well,' replied Monsieur Durand, 'let us find out. May we use your library, Louise?'

'Of course,' said Cecile's aunt. 'Do.'

There was a huge globe of the world there and when you pressed a button it was lit up from the inside. Cecile and her father looked at this to find first France and then Paris. With his finger, Monsieur Durand drew an imaginary airline from Paris down the boot of Italy to Athens, the capital of Greece, from there across the Mediterranean to Cairo, the chief city of Egypt. Then they followed the wriggling River Nile into the heart of Ethiopia where Cecile read the name of its capital, Addis Ababa.

So that's where Jean-Pierre was! Some six inches and more than three thousand miles away on the face of the globe, but at least SOMEWHERE.

And not only somewhere, but in good hands, looked after, cared for and loved by someone. Her heart went out to the unknown Abo Tenawayo. 'He said he was an Amhara boy, Papa, what's that?'

'Supposing we see if we can find one,' said Monsieur

Durand. He took down a book and turned to a page on which was a picture of a good-looking, brown-skinned boy with flashing eyes and white teeth. He was wearing a striped blanket.

'Is that Abo?' Cecile asked.

'No, but he will look like that. The Amharas are the principal people of Abyssinia. They are a proud and handsome race, strong and brave.'

'And kind,' Cecile added. 'He gave Jean-Pierre his warm milk and a kiss. But why did they laugh and say they had never seen anyone like him before? It's where he came from, isn't it?'

Monsieur Durand replied, 'Well, now, we'd better find out about that, too.'

'Hello,' he cried, 'here's a surprise!' and read out, '"The so-called Abyssinian Guinea Pigs have no connection with Abyssinia, but they have coarse hair forming whorls and rosettes—" that means going every-which-way.'

He put his finger on the continent of South America on the globe. 'Actually, all Guinea Pigs came originally from here,' he said.

'Then why is he called "Abyssinian"?' Cecile persisted.

Monsieur Durand thought hard for a moment. 'It's one of those things in life that have no explanation,' he said. 'Sometimes articles are called by what they aren't. Scotch tape wasn't invented in Scotland; they don't eat hamburgers in Hamburg and Great Dane dogs don't come from Denmark. Perhaps it was because this kind of Guinea Pig's hair was kinky, like that of the Abyssinians.'

Cecile was satisfied with this. It didn't really matter to her whether Jean-Pierre had actually come from Abyssinia or not. He was magic and special and that was that. Besides which, the other place her father had pointed out on the globe looked just as interesting. She would find out about that some other day.

She turned back to the letter once more. 'What does he mean by the "Glorios Emperer"?'

They found him in a third book, not only the Emperor, a dark, royal, bearded man wearing a cape, but two of his lions as well. They were photographed in the very palace gardens at Addis Ababa about which Abo had written.

One was lying at his feet and the other was rubbing up against his leg like a big cat.

'That's the Emperor Haile Selassie, a fine and courageous man.'

Cecile's eyes grew larger as she looked at the two fierce animals.

'But what are the lions for?'

'To guard him.'

'But Abo said that the lion ran away from Jean-Pierre.'

Monsieur Durand smiled and said, 'Yes, sometimes large animals are upset by very small ones. You know an elephant is supposed to be scared of a mouse, though I don't know how true that is.'

Cecile laughed suddenly, for the first time since her pet had been lost. For in her mind she was transported to the palace gardens of Addis Ababa. She saw the huge lion bending down to have a sniff at Jean-Pierre, and Jean-Pierre lifting up his head, his little pink nose twitching, as he sniffed right back, and the lion turning tail and galloping away. She was thrilled and proud. Her little friend had actually frightened a lion supposed to protect the Emperor. Probably it was one of those very ones there in the picture before her.

'I think it was just because he was so brave and magic, too,' she said. Much of her sadness and worry was lifted from her.

And just at that moment the telephone rang. This time it *was* for Cecile and it was indeed the airline confirming that the lost Guinea Pig had been traced to Addis Ababa. They explained how it had happened and informed her that now he would be on his way home. Cecile ought to have him by the following morning.

The next day, however, there was no Jean-Pierre, but only another letter.

chapter three

The day before, Cecile had been listening for the telephone to ring to bring her news of Jean-Pierre. This morning was one of waiting for the door bell. She pictured herself flinging open the door and receiving the precious travelling box with Jean-Pierre inside it.

The bell rang. Cecile rushed. But it was only the old postman. He said, 'Good morning, Mademoiselle. Here are four letters for Madame Tissaud and one for you.'

Cecile ran back into the room shouting, 'Papa, Mama, Aunt Louise! It isn't Jean-Pierre, it's only another letter from him.'

Her aunt glanced at the envelope and said, 'Why, it's from Karachi in Pakistan. My husband and I were in that part of the world for several years before he died. Perhaps

it's about your Guinea Pig again. Do open it and see what it says.' By now she was as interested as any of them in the strange fate of Jean-Pierre.

Cecile did this, being careful not to spoil the beautiful stamp. This letter proved to be in French. Her mother, father and aunt looking over her shoulder, all read together:

Karachi Airport,
Karachi,
Pakistan

Honoured Mademoiselle-Sahib,

Am well educated Babu, learned in French and English. I have read your instructions for your little Guinea Pig, Jean-Pierre, who has been sent here from Addis Ababa, where he was despatched in error. How sad for you!

I am employed as Chief of Baggage Department at airport here in Karachi. This is most important airport for all East–West Traffic. This is why your pet was forwarded here, to make connections. I am charged to put your friend on three o'clock plane for Paris.

I have thought long how to give proper food and care for him in night, but most important, love, as you have written in your letter. Food is simple. Difficult to find is the warm heart in this unhappy world.

I am reminded then of old and venerable Holy Man who sit under pipal tree at edge of airport and acquire great merit through prayer and goodness. You would be pleased. He have long white beard and beautiful eyes. To him I did entrust Jean-Pierre.

It was great success. Holy Man press him to his breast and pray with him, and many people come to look and give food and money. Never have they seen such a strange *chela*, and they venerate him along with Holy Man.

Soon the bowl of the Holy Man is overflowing. There was warm buffalo milk for Jean-Pierre and many annas and pice for Holy Man, which make him glad. He was loath to let Jean-Pierre go home, until I tell him the little one must return to you. Then he give his blessing and say goodbye.

So all is well and now I occupy myself with placing Jean-Pierre aboard Air India plane named *Bombay*.

Wishing good health to you and your family and relations and soon to be reunited.

Humble and respectfully,
Bowani-Singh.
Chief Baggage Master Karachi Airport.

PS So terribly sorry. Sudden airport strike this morning make impossible sending Jean-Pierre as planned. Do not despair! Eastward flight BOAC unaffected and have arranged for him to pick up KLM plane for Paris at Bangkok. He have departed for there in good health.

Faithfully,
B.
Chief B-M, KA

Cecile had been silent all through the letter, only her eyes growing larger and larger with interest. But when she came to the postscript she gave a cry of despair, 'He's gone to Bangkok! Where's that? Oh, Papa, hurry! Hurry!' And she was off in a flash to the library where she switched on the light in the big globe and searched. By the time her aunt and parents came into the room, she had found it.

'Papa,' she wailed, 'look! Jean-Pierre's even further away than before!'

This was indeed the case, as anyone with half an eye could see. Bangkok was the capital of Siam, or Thailand as it is called on the new maps, and lay some twelve inches away from Paris on the big globe. It was quite out of sight of that city, around a curve of the earth, some six thousand miles away.

Cecile began to cry. As a child of today she knew that the jet planes could span the miles in hours that formerly took weeks and even months to travel. But never had the world seemed so enormous to her, and distances so terrifying as at that moment. She looked upon the great land masses of Europe, Africa and Asia and thought of one tiny, helpless Guinea Pig wandering lost amongst them.

Monsieur Durand grew angry again, for this affair was now truly upsetting their holiday. 'This is an outrage!' he declared. 'I'm going to telephone the airline and give them a piece of my mind. This letter was dated two days ago. Goodness knows where the beast is by now.' He left the room.

Madame Tissaud, who loved her niece and could not bear to see her unhappy, put her arms about her and said, 'You mustn't cry, Cecile. Look, Jean-Pierre seems to fall into the hands of friends wherever he goes. He has been extraordinarily fortunate in Karachi. Read the letter again and you will see. It isn't everyone's Guinea Pig who gets to be the *chela* of a Holy Man in India.'

Cecile dried her tears and did as her aunt suggested. She read the letter the second time with more care. Now she had the strangest feeling of something sweet and tender in it.

'What is a Babu, Aunt Louise?' she asked.

Her aunt replied, 'A Babu is a clerk in India. They are sad little men with just enough education to puff them up and not sufficient to permit them to become really important. Jean-Pierre touched his heart, you can see. Bowani-Singh read your letter and saw that the animal was lost and lonely. The Babu too, feels lost and lonely in a world in which often there is no place for him.'

Cecile did not quite understand everything her aunt was saying, but she felt it had something to do with the sweetness and sadness that had come through the letter. The Baggage Master must be a busy man and yet he had occupied himself with a lost Guinea Pig.

'Why does the Holy Man sit under a pipal tree?' Cecile asked. 'And what is a pipal tree, Aunt Louise? – Oh, and what is a *chela*, too?'

There was sorrow in Madame Tissaud. She was remembering many things of long ago and a happier life she had once lived. She replied:

'A pipal tree is enormous, with a large trunk which is sometimes cracked and split. You might even go inside one and be sheltered from the sun, as though it were a cave. They have leaves that shake and shiver and dance in the breeze. The Holy Man sits in the shade at the foot of the tree with his begging bowl. This is what he looks like.'

She went to a cabinet and took out a photograph album which she opened. 'Here is a picture of one I took myself.'

It was somewhat faded, but Cecile could see an old man. He was wearing nothing but a white cloth around his middle and sitting cross-legged in the dust beneath a huge tree. There was an empty wooden bowl beside him. He had a flowing white beard which reached halfway to the ground and even from the photograph Cecile could see his eyes. They were indeed deep and mysterious.

'Oh, look,' she cried, 'a monkey!' For she had seen a little face peering out from the leaves of the tree.

'Yes,' said Madame Tissaud, 'they feed the monkeys and birds, for they love all little animals.'

'What else does he do?' Cecile asked.

'He meditates – which means thinking beautiful thoughts. Sometimes these holy men have a pupil who is close to them and he is called a *chela.* That's why the Babu said that Jean-Pierre had become a *chela* to the Holy Man and was venerated with him. When you know English better, you must read a book called *Kim* by Rudyard Kipling.'

Cecile studied the picture and thought it was strange that whereas a moment ago she had been shedding tears of grief, now she felt quite calm. Jean-Pierre had been held to the bosom of one of these men. What a wonderful thing for him! 'What does "venerated" mean?' she asked.

Her aunt reflected. 'It means to have respect for; to look up to. They regard the Holy Man with respect and awe, as a friend of the gods. And because of the good life he leads, they bring him food and money. Bowani-Singh writes there was warm buffalo milk for Jean-Pierre and annas and pice, which is Indian money like our francs and centimes, for the Holy Man. Cattle, you know, are worshipped as sacred in India. Perhaps because he was with the Holy Man, people thought Jean-Pierre was sacred, too.'

Cecile was not at all surprised at this, for wasn't Jean-Pierre magic as well as very special?

Her father came stumping back into the room. 'The idiots!' he exclaimed. 'They haven't a clue what has happened to him since he left Karachi, bound in the wrong direction. I told them what I thought of them and they are going to telephone through to Bangkok to try to find out where he is.'

'Perhaps there'll be another letter tomorrow,' put in Cecile's mother.

There wasn't. It came only the morning after.

chapter four

There was another beautiful stamp on the envelope and it came from the Kingdom of Thai. The handwriting was small, delicate and easy to read. In perfect French it began:

Dear Mademoiselle Durand,

I am writing to tell you of your little Guinea Pig, who was entrusted to my care until we were able to put him on a TWA plane for Paris, to be returned to you. You must be a very kind little girl to love your pet so much and leave such perfect instructions in case he should become lost.

He was given to me because I, too, own many pets. My name is Sirima Desjardins, and I am Siamese. My husband, Marcel, is French. He is Chief European Assistant to the Royal Forestry Department and is in charge of more than one hundred elephants.

I am sure you would be interested in my pets. I have a python (he is sweet and also likes to drink warm milk) and a dwarf deer; a ruffed lemur who would make you laugh, he looks so funny, and a honey bear. Jean-Pierre visited my python and played with the lemur. I also have my favourite elephant on which I ride. Her name is 'Nang-Hiaw', which means 'Old Wrinkled-Skin', and indeed her grey hide looks like the map of a thousand rivers. If you have never seen an elephant you must ask your parents to take you to the zoo. There you will also see what my other pets look like as well. I own many Siamese cats too, but of course you will have seen these.

But I have also a much wilder and larger animal. He is a fishing cat. He is something like a cheetah. His paws are lightning fast. He can whip a fish out of a stream before it even knows he is there. Perhaps your zoo will have one of these. I know there is a python there, because our King presented one to the Zoological Gardens of Paris.

Yesterday morning, after I fed Jean-Pierre, I took him on Nang-Hiaw (for some twenty of my husband's elephants are working on the edge of the airport here) and I think he liked it. I held him tightly to my cheek all the time. He wasn't frightened even when Nang touched him with the sensitive tip of her trunk. He only wrinkled up his nose and sneezed.

When we returned to the airport, the King and Queen of our country had just flown in from the north and Jean-Pierre saw them both. Queen Sirikit is the most lovely creature in the world, I am sure. She has exquisite and delicate features. When I see her she always makes me think of a frangipani flower. As they came down the steps from the aeroplane we all cheered and Nang-Hiaw saluted them with her trunk. They waved to us and to Jean-Pierre too.

Then I returned Jean-Pierre to the Director of the airport who put him aboard a TWA airliner bound for Paris. Perhaps you will have him back safe in your arms even before this letter arrives. But I thought you would like to know how he spent his time in our lovely country.

Wishing him a safe journey and a happy arrival,

Yours in distant friendship

Sirima Desjardins

PS I enclose for you a little snapshot of myself taken with some of my pets.

S.D.

Royal Forestry Service,
Bangkok, Thailand

Cecile was simply breathless with excitement after she had finished the letter and they had all examined the photo.

'Oh, isn't she beautiful!' she gasped. 'And look at all her animals.'

There in the midst of a tropical garden like a jungle, stood a tiny woman. With black hair and almond-shaped eyes, she looked like a little doll. She wore silk trousers and an embroidered jacket.

Down from the branch of a tree overhead, hung a huge snake. But its head was resting on one of her shoulders and it had a pleased expression. Lying at her feet on its back, was an enormous creature like a cat. It had dark brown stripes on its side and seemed to be waving its paws in the air. On her other shoulder wandered a Siamese kitten. Behind her loomed up an elephant, with a little brown man in a loin-cloth perched on its neck.

'An elephant!' Cecile cried. 'Jean-Pierre has ridden an elephant! Oh Papa, could we go to the zoo and see one? And what is the Royal Forestry Service? And a python? Oh, I do so want to go to the zoo and see all the animals Jean-Pierre met.'

Her father explained that the Royal Foresters in Thailand were in charge of all the work elephants who pushed and pulled the huge teak logs about.

But Cecile's mother said, 'What a good idea to go and see them.'

And so it was to the zoo at Vincennes they went off that day. The library could offer nothing as exciting as the living creatures.

'When you come home,' her Aunt Louise had said, 'I'll take you to tea with my friend Madame Lebrun, who lives next door. She has two lovely Siamese cats and you will be able to play with them.'

They first went to see the elephants and since it was a warm summer's day, the huge beasts were out in the open, standing in the shade of some rocks, blowing sand over their backs. Cecile had a bag of peanuts and when one wise old animal saw this out of the corner of her eye, she came galumphing over and held out her trunk.

Now Cecile could see exactly what Madame Sirima had meant by the map of a thousand rivers. This, too, was an old one and her hide was lined and wrinkled. But her eyes were very knowing and had long lashes.

She held out her trunk as straight as a ruler, opened her mouth and made little sucking noises. Cecile was afraid and threw the peanut on the ground. Then she watched the marvellous delicacy with which the huge elephant picked up the tiny peanut. She used the very tip of her trunk. Cecile remembered that this was what had tickled the end of Jean-Pierre's nose and made him sneeze.

And to think that Jean-Pierre had been for a ride on the back of such a tremendous animal! When the elephant saw there were to be no more peanuts, she went away. Cecile watched how her back swayed. She thought that riding an elephant must be something like being on a boat in a storm at sea and hoped that Jean-Pierre had not felt sick.

In the reptile house she saw a python coiled about the branches of an artificial tree. It was larger than the one in the photograph and as thick around as Cecile's two legs together, with a brown, mottled back and patterns of black markings. He seemed to be fast asleep, except once when he opened his eyes and stared at Cecile. For an instant the thin, double-ended fork of a tongue flickered from his mouth and Cecile thought that he winked at her before the heavy lids, like scales, descended over the beady eyes again.

She read the sign at the bottom of the cage, '*Python Reticulatus*. Habitat Malay Region. Presented by HRH King Bhumibol of Thailand'.

There it was, exactly as Madame Sirima had written! And Jean-Pierre had seen the King as well.

The ruffed lemur was just as funny as Madame Sirima had said. It wasn't really a monkey, but it wasn't *not* a monkey either. It was dressed in black and white fur and looked like nothing so much as a sleepy circus clown.

Cecile would not have exchanged Jean Pierre for any of these, but it was plain to see why Madame Sirima liked having them as pets. The dwarf deer had the most sweet, liquid, trusting eyes. The honey bear was cuddly as her own teddy at home. And while there was no fishing cat in the zoo, the cheetah which it was supposed to be like looked so noble that Cecile wished she could take its soft head in her arms and hug it.

But of course these were not all the animals that she and her family saw on that delightful day.

They had a long look at the African lions. Amongst them was a fine fellow with a black mane, just like the ones in the picture with Haile Selassie. Once again Cecile trembled at the bravery of her tiny pet to stand his ground and sniff back at such a terrifying brute, and make it turn tail and run.

They marvelled at the giraffe, the ugly rhinoceros and hippopotamus and the most unusual of all the animals, the kangaroos. One of them was carrying a baby in her pouch. Cecile shouted with delight to see the little head peering forth. Her father explained to her that this was how these strange beasts, known as *Marsupials*, fed and protected their young.

They could have spent a whole week in the monkey house, watching the antics of the chimpanzees and the long-armed gibbons, flying like circus acrobats from one end of their cages to the other.

When the day was over, they went directly to Madame Lebrun's house for tea. Here Aunt Louise awaited them and introduced Cecile to her friend's two Siamese cats, Sarit and Sarat.

They were the most gorgeous creatures with fur the colour of tea-with-milk, china blue eyes and little black faces. They had browny-black feet and their tails had a funny kink. Their voices were strange too, like the cry of a baby. When they played with Cecile they behaved more like dogs than cats, romping and racing up and down the room with her. They scampered and leaped from one piece of furniture to another, up on to the mantel, over the sofa and side tables, without ever upsetting a single thing. What with the cats and Madame Sirima, and all the animals, Cecile thought that Thailand must indeed be a wonderful country that she would like to visit sometime. How fortunate Jean-Pierre was to have been there.

Cecile wanted to go home in case Jean-Pierre should be there waiting for her. And she *didn't* want to go home, in case he wasn't and by staying away she might still give him time to arrive before she did.

But eventually the moment came to leave. She kissed Sarit and Sarat good-bye on top of their cold noses. Then impatiently she tugged at her father's hand during the short walk home, to make him hurry.

Jean-Pierre hadn't arrived.

Instead there was another letter. This time it was a Special Delivery AIRMAIL. The postman had brought it on a motor-bike and the maid had signed for it. It was almost covered with foreign stamps and a large label with the word EXPRESS printed on it.

When Cecile opened it, she received the greatest fright she had ever had in her whole life. It was more severe even than the day she had come home from school to find that Jean-Pierre had been pignapped.

chapter five

Here is what Monsieur Durand translated for her from its stiff official English:

Superintendent's Office,
Paya Lebar International Airport,
Singapore

Dear Miss Durand,

Having seen the general signal put out by the airlines concerning the misdirection of your Guinea Pig, I must say I was not too surprised when he turned up here aboard a Westbound Trans-World plane from Bangkok. It was diverted because of a dangerous cyclone reported over the Bay of Bengal, and forced to land here until the weather cleared. Your pet was off-loaded and brought to my office.

Since you will probably have read the papers, I am writing to you to say not to worry about him during the spot of trouble here with the Indonesians. It was sticky for a time, but seems now to be quieted down, with our troops in control.

However, as soon as the firing began I was certain they were trying for the airport. With Qantas Flight 903 loaded and about to taxi to the line for its scheduled take-off to Sydney, Australia, I rushed Jean-Pierre aboard, rather than risk his being injured during the shooting, which became rather heavy at one time.

He is a calm little Guinea Pig and never turned a hair when a mortar shell knocked a bit of a hole through the wall of my office; he only sneezed a good deal, more likely from the dust raised than anything else. But it then seemed to me time to get him out of here, if you were ever to see him again. It's done now and I have advised Sydney to put him on the next plane for Paris, so he'll be back with you before long. Sorry you've had this further delay.

Yours sincerely,

A. E. Stoddard, DSO, MC

Superintendent,

Paya Lebar International Airport,

Singapore

When her father finished Cecile grew pale and her lips began to tremble as large tears formed in her eyes. The letter had been very grown-up and she had not completely understood. Yet it was clear enough to her that there had been shooting and an explosion of some kind, and that Jean-Pierre had been in terrible danger.

While Cecile and her school friends had enough work and play to occupy them, they were nevertheless aware that there was always some kind of fighting going on somewhere in the world. They would catch a glimpse of a picture in the newspaper, or see it on television.

No one paid a great deal of attention to these distant battles that really did not affect them. But here was one that most certainly did concern Cecile closely. Suddenly Jean-Pierre had been in the midst of it. A pignapping was one thing, for while there was life, there was always hope. But when you were shot, or blown up, that was the end.

'Jean-Pierre! Oh, my poor Jean-Pierre!' cried Cecile and began to sob again.

'No, no!' her father said, 'Stop it! There's nothing to

cry about. Don't you see? He's quite safe! But this is most remarkable. I seem to remember now. Louise, have you the newspapers from two or three days ago?'

Cecile's aunt went into the kitchen and dug into a cupboard where they were kept. And sure enough there was the item about an unsuccessful raid on the airport at Singapore.

'Your little Guinea Pig has found a friend again,' Monsieur Durand explained. 'And this time a kind and gallant man. Do you see those letters after his name? They stand for decorations for bravery he received as an officer in the last World War.'

Cecile's father too had known his share of wars and had been under fire. This time it was *he* who was using his

imagination. He could see it almost, the attack in the early morning and the hole knocked through the Superintendent's office before one knew what was happening. He could smell the smoke and hear the rattling of machine-guns and the whistle and whine of the bullets. In his mind he saw the Superintendent march fearlessly through the shot criss-crossing the airport. Sheltering the box against his body he clapped Jean-Pierre aboard the waiting aeroplane and waved them off. And all for a child far away, whom he did not even know.

Monsieur Durand retold it like a story to Cecile. She dried her eyes and thought that never in the whole world could there have been a Guinea Pig who had managed to live through such adventures. Where, then, was he now and what could the next one be?

When she hurried to the library to see where Australia and Sydney were, her heart sank again. For not only were

they more inches and many more thousands of miles away from France, but actually tucked away on the DOWN-UNDER side of the globe so that she had to bend low to see them.

For all of the exciting time he must be having, the fact was that Jean-Pierre was also managing to get himself further and further away from home.

Yet it was in Australia that Jean-Pierre really had his strangest experience. And it provided Cecile with quite the most exciting moment of the holiday.

chapter six

Since the next day was Sunday, there was of course no post, and hence no news of Jean-Pierre. It was an unhappy one for Cecile because, in addition to everything else, it was raining. The picnic and trip to Fontainebleau, which had been planned, had to be cancelled.

So, after lunch, Cecile rather sadly went into the library to look at the big globe once more. She touched the tiny spot marked Sydney on the vast continent of Australia. Then she looked at a picture of the city in a geography book. But it brought her no closer to her lost pet. She tried to read about the place, but it seemed very dull.

The telephone rang in the drawing-room. Cecile heard her father who answered it, saying in a loud voice, 'What? What? From where, did you say? My daughter, Cecile? You're sure it's for Mademoiselle Cecile Durand? Yes, yes, she's here! Hold on, I'll call her. Cecile, Cecile, where are you? Come here at once! It's for you, from Australia.'

From Australia! But that's where Jean-Pierre was!

She ran to the drawing-room where her father held out the receiver for her.

'It's for you. A personal call from Sydney,' he said. 'Now don't be too excited. You can hear clearly. We'll go upstairs and listen in on the extension in the bedroom.'

Strangely, now that it had come, Cecile was really quite calm. For she had felt sure that some time or other Jean-Pierre would work some more of his special magic.

Well, it wasn't exactly Jean-Pierre himself, but it was

so close as never mind. When she said, 'Hello,' a telephonist asked, 'Mademoiselle Cecile Durand on the line? Go ahead, Sydney.'

A man said in French: 'Hello, Cecile, can you hear me?'

Cecile replied that she could, for it was just as plain as though the call were coming from across the street.

'This is Mister Flippo speaking. Perhaps you have never heard of me, but I am a famous circus clown. Have you ever been to a circus?'

'Oh yes,' replied Cecile, 'often, when it comes to Cannes.'

'Good,' said Mister Flippo, 'then you'll understand. I have your little Guinea Pig, Jean-Pierre, right here with me, safe and sound. In a moment perhaps you can speak to him. But first you might like to know what's happened and why he's with me.'

Jean-Pierre right there! Cecile thought that she would die of excitement. But where was *there*? She looked at the black telephone instrument and then around the room for a moment. 'There' was a place on the other side of the earth, millions and millions of miles away.

Still, she remembered to be polite and said, 'Oh yes, please!'

'Well, here's the story,' began Mister Flippo at the other end. 'When Jean-Pierre arrived in Sydney nobody knew where he was from, or where he was going, or what to do with him. But when they read your clever little letter inside his cage, they knew that someone would have to look after him until they found out. And who do you think they went to? Old Mister Flippo, the circus clown, with his educated kangaroos and his trained pigs. They said, "If Mister Flippo can teach a pig to walk a tightrope with a silk hat balanced on the end of its nose, he will know what to do with one small Guinea Pig." Tee, hee, hee, hee, hee!' He burst into the strangest kind of giggle and Cecile had to laugh herself.

'Our circus is playing in an amusement park not far from the airport. So they sent the little fellow over to me. I fed him and gave him his warm milk and then, where do you think he spent the night?'

'Where?' Cecile asked, prepared for almost anything but certainly not for what he said next.

'In Angelique!'

'Where?'

'In Angelique,' repeated Mister Flippo. 'Angelique is one of my kangaroos. Have you ever seen a kangaroo?'

'Oh yes,' cried Cecile, 'I saw one yesterday, in the zoo. And she had a little one with its head sticking out of her middle.'

'That's it,' replied Mister Flippo. 'You see, my Angelique's baby died and she was unhappy. Jean-Pierre was lonely and cold, so that's exactly where I tucked him. They got on fine. And do you know what happened the next day?'

Cecile was almost breathless with excitement by now, but managed to say, 'No, what?'

'He looked so funny, the Guinea Pig, with his head sticking out of Angelique's pouch, that I put him in the act.'

'You mean Jean-Pierre was in the circus?' Cecile gasped.

'Right again!' said Mister Flippo. 'You're a clever girl. Tee, hee, hee, hee, hee!' And his shrill laughter came over the telephone once more from halfway around the world.

'He was a sensation! Three thousand children laughed, cheered and clapped when I took him out of Angelique's pouch and showed him to them. I shall have to get a Guinea Pig of my own. Oh, he was marvellous! Such stage presence! Like an old trouper. Well then, the next day they came from the airport to say that they had found out where he belonged and that he must go home. They said they would put a call through to you so I could tell you all about it. But we had one more performance together tonight, didn't we, Jean-Pierre old fellow? You see, it's midnight here and the show is just over.'

Cecile looked up at the clock on the mantel and saw that it was three in the afternoon in Paris. She already knew from her geography lessons that time changed when you were far away. Still it was most confusing.

'Speak to him, Cecile,' said Mister Flippo.

'Oh, Jean-Pierre, Jean-Pierre, Jean-Pierre!' Cecile cried into the telephone. 'Jean-Pierre, can you hear me?'

For a moment there was a silence from the other end of the line and then – could it be possible? She heard a faint little chirrup, followed by the tiniest noise of small teeth clicking together. They were actually Jean-Pierre noises that she knew so well. And then, best and most wonderful of all, in quick succession came three small but unmistakable Jean-Pierre sneezes.

'There you are!' It was Mister Flippo again. 'He said "Hello" to you. Tonight he will sleep in Angelique for the last time and early tomorrow, that's Monday morning, he is starting his journey back home to you. How's that?'

'Oh thank you, thank you, thank you, Mister Flippo!' said Cecile. 'I wish I knew what you looked like.'

'Me? Oh, I'm very silly! I have a white face and two crosses for eyes and a big red nose and mouth. I'll send you my picture and a picture of Jean-Pierre inside Angelique.' The shrill laugh came over for the last time. 'Tee, hee, hee, hee! Who ever before saw a Guinea Pig in the pouch of a kangaroo? *Au revoir*, Cecile, *au revoir*!'

Then there was a click at the other end of the line and it was over.

Cecile sat down on the floor beside the telephone and began to cry. But they were tears not of misery, but of excitement, wonder and happiness. What a tale she would have when she went back to school again! Had ever a little girl before talked to her Guinea Pig held in the arms of a clown on the down-under side of the earth? Or owned a Guinea Pig who had slept inside the pouch of a kangaroo and been a part of a circus in far-off Sydney, Australia?

The others came into the room and Monsieur Durand said, 'There now, Cecile, what do you think of that?'

'He spoke to me, Papa! Did you hear him? He said he was coming home to me.'

'Well, I certainly heard him sneeze,' Monsieur Durand

said, 'if nothing else. And now, you know, you needn't worry any more.'

He had reason to feel pleased with himself. For while he had never expected such a thing as a telephone call from Australia, in a way it was he who was responsible. The night before he had rung the airline and given them a proper piece of his mind.

He had told them that while it was not their fault that there had been a strike in Karachi, a cyclone over the Bay of Bengal and a revolution at Singapore, if they hadn't sent Jean-Pierre off to Abyssinia in the first place none of this would have happened. If they had put him on the Caravelle from Nice to Paris where he belonged, he wouldn't be in Sydney, or goodness knows where now.

The airline man had been as astounded as the Durands to learn that Jean-Pierre somehow had got himself to Australia and had promised they would do everything possible to straighten matters out.

That night, of all things, Cecile asked to go to bed early. She wanted to think by herself.

She had been back to the library to look over the tremendous spaces through which her speech and the sounds of Jean-Pierre had travelled in the smallest part of a second. It was hard to understand how her voice in Paris had just had lunch, but in Sydney would be fast asleep. She needed to be alone because when there are grown-ups about it is difficult to imagine things properly.

When at last her mother kissed her goodnight and put out the light, she could begin.

She saw then the circus ring as she remembered it, when the Bouglioni Brothers or the Circus Knie came to Cannes, and the music of the red-coated band was in her ears. She imagined Mister Flippo in his clown's costume and pointed hat, with crosses on his white-painted face

where his eyes should be, and the funny red nose. She had never seen a pig balance a silk hat, but there it was now, all in her mind. Then the kangaroo came in hippety-hop, sitting on its long tail. Looking out from the pouch at its middle was the face of Jean-Pierre. And on this she lingered, hearing the shouts, laughter, the applause and the cries of delight from the audience, until she fell asleep.

But the adventures of the little Guinea Pig were not yet over. For he had still to work his greatest and most astonishing piece of magic – abracadabra and presto-bambo! The changing of Monday into Sunday! It was something no other Guinea Pig had ever done before.

chapter seven

It began the very next morning with the arrival of a cablegram addressed to Cecile. This in itself was a novel and exciting affair. She had never had a cablegram or even a telegram before. Her mother explained it was a message sent from far off by wire.

It was delivered by a special man in a blue and red uniform. Before he would hand it over, Cecile had to sign her name in his book. This she did carefully and neatly, even though her hand was shaking slightly. What on earth had Jean-Pierre been up to now?

A cablegram is not at all like a letter in France. It arrives on a piece of blue paper merely folded over and gummed.

It was difficult for Cecile even to make head or tail of it

at first, for it was all in capital letters with no punctuation marks. There were also some letters and figures above the message part that made no sense to her at all. Since it was in English her father read it and translated it for her as follows:

YOUR GUINEA PIG JEAN-PIERRE STOPPED OFF HERE INTERNATIONAL AIRPORT HONOLULU EN ROUTE PARIS VIA SAN FRANCISCO NEW YORK STOP IN ADDITION THINGS YOU WROTE HE LIKED TO EAT HE ALSO GOES FOR PINEAPPLE PAPAYA COCONUT BREADFRUIT YAMS MALAY AND CUSTARD APPLES AVOCADOS POI MANGOES GUAVA POHA TAMARIND PASSION FRUIT LICHEE MACADAMIA NUTS AND SUGAR CANE ALL PRODUCTS HAWAIIAN ISLANDS STOP HE ENJOYED SOME OF EACH ONLY HOPE NOT GIVE HIM STOMACH ACHE STOP DEPARTED HERE OKAY GOOD WISHES SAFE ARRIVAL Y A CHIN TRAFFIC SUPERINTENDENT INTERNATIONAL AIRPORT HONOLULU.

This, of course, led to an immediate rush for the now familiar reference books. What she found resulted in another outburst from Cecile.

'Oh, Papa, he's going even further from us!' For the Hawaiian Islands and their capital, Honolulu, were in the middle of the Pacific Ocean.

'Actually, he isn't,' Monsieur Durand explained. 'They're just sending him around the other way. If you look at a flat map of the world it's confusing. But see here on the globe which is round, as the earth is, it's as fast by airline one way as the other. Probably they put him on the first plane out which happened to be going in that direction.'

The cablegram was full of words and things that Cecile had never heard of before, such as all the tropical fruits. Monsieur Durand promised to go to a speciality shop to buy some for them to try, coconuts, yams – which were sweet potatoes – custard apples which tasted like cheap scent; avocados, also known as alligator pears from their rough, wrinkled skin, and the lichee nuts with their strange, juicy interiors. They looked up Hawaii and saw pictures of those beautiful Islands.

Cecile came back to the figures and letters at the beginning of the cablegram and wanted to know what they meant. Her father sat down to puzzle them out.

They read: EX OAHU INT AIR HONOLULU 20:15 HRS WPT 25/7/65 ARR PARIS CENT 07:00 HRS 26/7/65.

Monsieur Durand was willing to try anything if it would help Cecile to understand things. And so he took a scribbling-pad and pencil and after a few minutes he said to her, 'Here we are, I think. Oahu is the Hawaiian Island on which the capital, Honolulu, is situated. Well then, the cable was handed in by Mr Chin at the International Airport in Honolulu at a quarter past eight, Western Pacific Ocean Time, on Sunday night, the 25th of July. It was received at the Paris Central Office at seven o'clock this Monday morning.'

Cecile was regarding what he had written down on the pad with such a puzzled expression on her face that Monsieur Durand felt it necessary to try to explain further.

'These are all abbreviations,' he said. '"Ex" means "from", for instance. "WPT" stands for "Western Pacific Time" and of course you know the way of writing dates: 25/7/65 means the twenty-fifth day of the seventh month of this year, which was Sunday.'

'But Papa,' Cecile said, 'there must be a mistake.'

'Mistake?'

Cecile was bright and observant and always tried to put two and two together. When things didn't seem to add up, she wanted to know why and had been taught to ask.

'It couldn't be Sunday,' she said, 'because it was Sunday when Mister Flippo telephoned and he said Jean-Pierre was leaving on Monday. How could he arrive the day before he left?'

Monsieur Durand examined the dates on the cablegram again and said, 'Hello! You're right. It must be an error.'

Then, suddenly he laughed aloud. 'But of course,' he said, 'he's crossed the International Date Line and by going eastwards has gained a full day.'

Quite naturally Cecile asked, 'What's the International Date Line, Papa?' for she had not understood a word of what he said.

Monsieur Durand knew that it was going to be difficult to explain. But always when Cecile asked a question he tried to answer it.

'Come here,' he said and they went back to the globe. He showed her a dotted, red line wandering down from the North to the South Pole, through the middle of the Pacific Ocean. The words 'International Date Line' were printed on it. 'When you're a little older, you'll learn at school why time is different in Australia from what it is in France, due to the movement of the earth around the sun. To make it come out even, this is an imaginary line people have agreed upon. When you cross it travelling eastwards, you gain a day. When you cross it travelling in the other direction, you lose a day. But not to worry your head about it, you're still too young to understand.'

Cecile thought for a moment and then said, 'Oh, but I do understand, Papa.'

'Splendid!' said Monsieur Durand, quite proud of his daughter. 'You're a clever little girl.'

'It's Jean-Pierre's magic,' Cecile declared. 'He wanted to come home to me more quickly and so he changed Monday back into Sunday. He's the only Guinea Pig in the world who could change Monday to Sunday, or Friday to Thursday, or any other day if he felt like it. Isn't that true, Papa?'

Monsieur Durand thought for a moment and then said, 'Do you know, for the time being I think that your explanation is as good as any and I'm prepared to accept it. And if he's that magic, you oughtn't to worry about him any longer. He'll manage.'

Cecile nodded and then added, 'But I wouldn't like Jean-Pierre to get a tummy ache.'

For if Jean-Pierre could be said to have a fault it was that he was a bit greedy. If allowed, he would eat and eat until his sides swelled out and one was afraid he would burst.

Unhappily he did get a stomach ache and it was most severe.

chapter eight

All those strange fruits gave him such a pain that the day he arrived in New York, attendants awaiting him at the airport were terrified to find a very sick and unhappy little Guinea Pig.

His nose was hot. His eyes were watery. His otherwise pretty, browny-black fur was damp and matted. He huddled in one corner of his cage, shivering and chittering miserably.

The officials were most worried, for the complaints of Monsieur Durand had gone right up to the president of the airline. He had sent special orders around the world that the lost animal must be found and restored to its owner immediately. What if it were to die, now that it had flown safely more than two-thirds of the way around the earth?

A consultation was called at the airport and a local veterinary was swiftly summoned.

He hemmed and hawed and looked as wise as he could. But he had never had an Abyssinian Guinea Pig as a patient before. Also he did not know the cause of this stomach ache or what he had eaten in Hawaii.

He could only advise that Jean-Pierre be kept warm and quiet and on a very light diet of well-warmed milk. Milk, unfortunately, was just the wrong thing.

The next day Jean-Pierre was no better, but even worse. The officials at the airport were now almost ill themselves with worry.

Then one of them remembered having read that there was a learned Professor Jones in New York, who had hundreds and hundreds of Guinea Pigs. He was studying them in order to write a book about them. If there was one man who knew all there was to know about what might be the matter with a Guinea Pig, it was this professor.

Hurried telephone calls were made. Then, in a special ambulance with a motor cycle escort of police, Jean-Pierre was rushed from the airport to the laboratory of Professor Jones in downtown New York.

Fortunately Cecile knew nothing of this. The people in

America did not even dare to let the president of the airline know what had happened. Nor did they wish to advise Cecile that Jean-Pierre seemed to be at the point of death and that if Professor Jones could not cure him, no one could.

And so once more for a matter of five days, Jean-Pierre vanished into the blue with nobody apparently able to trace hide nor hair of him.

Strange to say Cecile took this calmly and occupied herself with enjoying the rest of her holiday. For she was certain that a Guinea Pig who was magic enough to telephone her from Australia, and turn Monday back into Sunday would come safely home to her.

Not so Monsieur Durand, who grew more and more angry and kept telephoning every day. One night, in the privacy of the bedroom, he said to his wife, 'Well, my dear, I have found out from the airline president what has happened to Jean-Pierre and *he* only learned it a few hours ago. Jean-Pierre is very ill and some professor in New York is trying to save his life, but they think he is going to die.'

'Oh dear,' cried Madame Durand, 'Cecile will be heart-broken! She loves him so. What an awful thing to happen. What *are* we going to do?'

Monsieur Durand said, 'I don't know, but I think we ought to prepare her for it, don't you?'

Madame Durand sighed and said, 'Yes, I suppose so. It might be best if I did it.'

And so sometime during the next day, Cecile's mother put her arm around her and said, 'My darling, would you be very much upset if Jean-Pierre were never to come back?'

'Oh, but he will, Mummy,' said Cecile.

'But what if he didn't? Supposing something happened to him so far away?'

Cecile said, 'But how could it, Mummy? Jean-Pierre is magic. Don't you remember how he sent me a secret message when he was pignapped? And how he telephoned me from Australia? And how Papa said he changed Monday into Sunday? He's probably having another adventure somewhere. Perhaps he'll be at home waiting for me when we get there.'

Against such faith Madame Durand found that she could say no more.

And then the day for their return to the South of France was at hand. The holiday was over. They were all packed and ready to leave for the aeroplane back to Nice. There the head gardener would meet them with the car and drive them to the flower farm behind Cannes.

Fortunately it was Monsieur Durand who went down early to see about putting the bags in the taxi. And so it was he who met the postman with a final letter for Miss Cecile Durand.

On the outside of the envelope was printed, 'Professor R. G. Jones, Biological Research Department, New York University, Washington Square, New York'.

This could only be from the professor announcing the end of Jean-Pierre! At that moment Cecile came clattering down the stairs. So Monsieur Durand hastily tucked the envelope, unopened, into his pocket.

Aunt Louise came to the cab to see them off and listened to the final instructions from Cecile as to exactly what to do and how to look after Jean-Pierre, should he arrive at her house after they had departed.

Then the taxi drove off in the direction of Orly airport and the journey home began.

The flight was uneventful. Cecile looked dreamily out of her window watching the earth roll by beneath her. She saw the shining Alps to her left, the Rhône river, and noticed the flat fields turn to the crumpled, brown hills of the Alpes Maritimes. Then at last the blue Mediterranean was below them and the trip almost over.

Some of the time she wondered where Jean-Pierre might be flying at that moment.

Monsieur Durand was most uncomfortable. He felt that the fatal letter from New York was burning a hole in his pocket. But he was unable to have a look at it, for they were all sitting together.

The Caravelle made its gentle landing on the airstrip and taxied up to the white administration building. There it swung around and the roar of its jet engines came to an end.

People arose and made their way out through the rear of the plane and down the stairs. Since Cecile and her family had been sitting well in front, they were the last ones off.

They were all carrying books and parcels, gifts from Aunt Louise. These had to be divided up between them. So it was while arranging this by the steps of their own aircraft that they saw a most extraordinary performance.

A big Pan American four-engined jet Boeing had landed just before them. The passengers had already left it and the luggage was being unloaded. But four officials were standing uneasily by one compartment door that had not been opened.

Out from the airport building came a procession of

three limousines. They drove up and came to a halt beside the huge, transatlantic aeroplane.

From the first car stepped an important-looking man in civilian clothes. He was accompanied by four others in uniform, absolutely covered with gold braid. From the second car appeared two men who were obviously doctors, for they carried little black bags. And from the third car out marched three airline hostesses and a nursing sister.

'Goodness,' said Monsieur Durand, 'there must be someone very important and very ill aboard that plane.'

Cecile said, 'Oh, Papa, let's stay and watch a moment!'

As the important-looking man in civilian clothes approached, the four attendants waiting there snapped to attention. The doctors stepped up closer. The hostesses and the nurse stood at the ready. The man motioned for the compartment door to be opened. Up it flew. From inside it a hand passed out – a small box. Well, a kind of cage. It had so many labels and stickers on it the wood could hardly be seen, but at one end was a square of wire mesh and poking his pink, healthy nose up against it was...

'Jean-Pierre! Jean-Pierre!' screamed Cecile at the top of her lungs. She ran across the tarmac to the plane and threw her arms about the box, hugging it to her.

'Jean-Pierre, you've come back to me! I knew you would!'

All of those gathered around looked stunned and shocked. The important man cried, 'Here, here, young lady! You mustn't touch that!'

'But it's my Guinea Pig,' said Cecile. 'It's my Jean-Pierre who was lost. Look, he knows me.'

She opened the cage, reached inside and took him out. The Guinea Pig was overcome with joy at being back with Cecile again. He squealed, clicked, chirruped, shrieked and sneezed all at the same time, and then snuffled his way into her neck.

'Oh, *Mon Dieu*!' groaned the important-looking man and mopped his brow with a handkerchief.

At this moment Monsieur and Madame Durand came up.

'Are you Monsieur Durand, and is this Cecile?' the man asked.

'Yes, of course,' said Monsieur Durand. 'Would you like to see my passport to prove it?'

'No, no,' said the man, 'for heaven's sake take the animal. They were so nervous in New York they put him on the wrong plane again, the one that flies directly from New York to Nice. But we were notified and were preparing to meet him and forward him on to Paris on the next Caravelle. The president of the airline is furious. He said if anything happened to the beast he would have our heads off.'

Well, and there was Jean-Pierre in Nice, right back where he started from, except that he had travelled entirely around the world. The doctors, the nurse, the officials and the air hostesses got back into their cars and drove away with sighs of relief. Cecile, hugging Jean-Pierre, went to their car and soon they were on the road home.

‘Oh, and by the way,’ said Monsieur Durand, reaching into his pocket, ‘here is a last letter which came for you this morning. I – ah – forgot to give it to you before.’

It was a short one, written in English in the hand of a child. It was so simple that her father did not have to translate it for her. It said:

Dear Cecile,

My name is Mary-Lou Jones. My father is a famous professor. He has cured Jean-Pierre who is feeling better. I am ten years old and in 4th Grade. I thought Jean-Pierre would like to see New York. My mother and I took him up to the top of the Empire State Building. It has 86 floors. It is the highest building in the world. Jean-Pierre liked it. He is going home today. Please write to me and send me some French stamps.

Your Pen Pal,
Mary-Lou Jones

Monsieur and Madame Durand read the letter with Cecile and had to smile at their fears. They, too, should have believed with Cecile when she said that Jean-Pierre was magic.

*

That night, alone at last with Jean-Pierre in her own bedroom, in her own home, cuddling him in her arms, Cecile quite suddenly looked at him with astonishment.

This was her Jean-Pierre who had:

(1) Frightened a lion belonging to the Emperor of Abyssinia and had made it run away.

(2) Met a Babu, spent the night with a Holy Man under a pipal tree in Karachi and had been venerated.

(3) Ridden on an elephant, encountered a python, played with a lemur and seen the King and Queen of Thailand.

(4) Escaped from bombs and bullets in a revolution in Singapore.

(5) Slept inside a kangaroo and taken part in a circus with a real clown in Australia.

(6) Over-eaten in Honolulu.

(7) Been to the top of the world's tallest building in New York.

And the surprising thing was THAT HE DIDN'T LOOK ONE BIT DIFFERENT. You simply couldn't tell.

He was exactly the same Jean-Pierre who had left her two weeks ago; no bigger, no smaller, no fatter, no thinner.

Cecile looked again at the labels from the various airlines and places on his box. But even then it was hard to believe. She opened her geography book at the map of the world and matched the labels with the names she had already found on her aunt's globe.

There they were: Addis Ababa, Karachi, Bangkok, Singapore, Sydney, Honolulu and New York. Her little pet had been to all of them while she had been no further than Paris.

She held him up in her two hands and looked into his golden-yellow eyes and cried, 'Oh, Jean-Pierre, no other girl has ever had such a splendid and magic Guinea Pig! You're marvellous!!!'

Jean-Pierre sneezed happily six times in a row, to celebrate the happy end to his adventures.

Also by Paul Gallico

The Day Jean-Pierre Joined the Circus 35p

In this adventure, Jean-Pierre becomes a circus star. How he does and what happens as a result, involve all sorts of excitement and thrills.

Manxmouse 40p

Manxmouse is the only one of his kind, and his adventures from the day of his creation are unique. He survives tigers and elephants and his life seems to be charmed – until he meets Manx Cat.

Ann Lawrence

The Travels of Oggy 40p

Oggy, a hedgehog who thinks Hampstead Heath is the whole world, sets out to find his family (human) who have moved to the country. He meets many other creatures on his quest, endearing himself to all of them and having some wonderfully funny adventures.